For A.

the
unexpected
journey

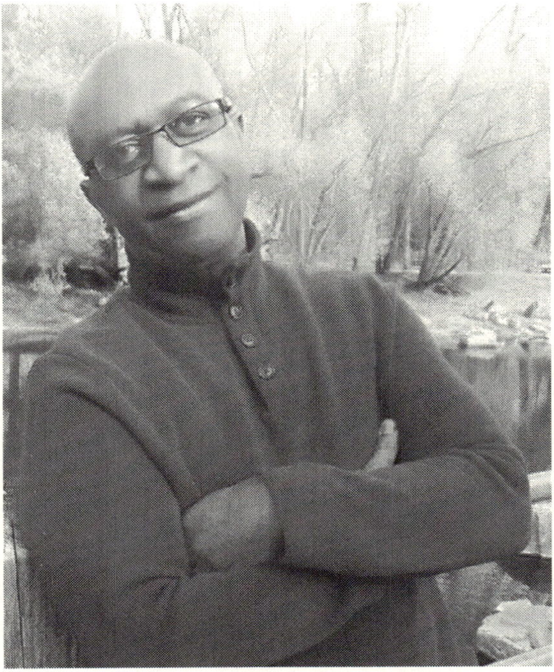

THE UNEXPECTED JOURNEY
copyright © 2020 by stewart sealy
all rights reserved
no part of this book may be used or reproduced in any manner
whatsoever without written permission except in the case of brief
quotations embodied in critical articles and reviews
for more information, email author

cover created by leta taylor (www.spacesofarcadia.com)

email iamstewartsealy@gmail.com
instagram @iamstewartsealy

also by the author

listen 2 the future

the
unexpected
journey

**stewart
sealy**

preface

no one picks up a book and expects to stay in the
same place as they were before
mentally
emotionally
and spiritually

my hope
is as you pick up this book
that it is not merely pages and ink
but that you fill it with your own story
and that you would read between the lines

this book is for those that are daring as a lion
to redesign their lives
rediscover their purpose
and reconnect to missed opportunities

it is for the ones working towards the best version
of themselves
even after the unexpected journey has you smack in
the middle of your greatest adversity

do not expect others to understand
do not bank on someone else to save you
this is your moment to use your faith and believe in
yourself

there are no right
or wrong answers in this book

do not judge yourself if you are a victim for over-
loving
and do not condemn yourself
if you have hurt someone else in your weakness
self-forgiveness is healing

may this book motivate
inspire
and empower

this is my way of speaking to myself

Stewart Sealy

the next time you see me

i will be the diamond that someone else has found

success won't be wishful thinking

or a collection of self-help quotes
stuck on the walls

dedication

i dedicate this book to my four awesome boys
my brother
and my sisters
that have always been there for me

and to all those
that did not expect to start over
but found the will to rise to a new
extraordinary
future in the making

contents

opportunity
the storm 3
time travel 4
nothing is what it seems 5
the struggle 6
you be 7
addictions 8
seldom 9
the mystery 10
imagine 11-12
intelligent design 13
the crisis 14
the future 15
forward thinking 16
why you 17-18
www 19
baggage 20
red flower 21
find the door 22
free 23
can you see it 24
the monster of fear 25
a hero 26

in
ihumans 28
future minds 29
tea with a friend 30
the storm before the calm 31
if i had wealth 32
drop the gun 33
year 3000 34
the fine line 35-36
next time 37-38
keep life simple 39
invisible 40

contents

forbidden fruit 41
a windy day 42
ready 43
remember 44
why 45
frog soup 46
wrong advice 47
electric blender 48
alone 49
overtake 50
flowers on the bench 51
double meaning 52
paradox 53
different kind 54
twenty-first century 55-56
your choice 57
next level 58
price paid 59
betrayal 60
you got this 61
okay the challenge 62
permission to win 63
the stage 64
all is not lost 65
upside down pages 66
when we find our why 67
know thy self 68
too scared 69
strange mystery 70-71
secrets 72
chips 73-74
agendas 75
pieces of yesterday 76
parallel 77
brown sugar 78

contents

all
frozen 80
a strange day 81
who can tell 82
you don't understand 83
the last day 84
framed 85
secrets again 86
bleeding doves 87
talking drums 88
ghetto 89
puppets 90
dust yourself off 91
is this for real 92-93
black privilege 94
mistake 95
executive decision 96-97
the last day of my past 98
relationship 99
four years later 100
persuasion 101
divine balance 102-103
lion in the street 104
no rush 105
game of hearts 106
final love 107
she 108
in the hood 109
glitter but is it gold 110
reach 111
flipside 112
missing in action 113
earth angel 114
inner world 115
no one left 116

contents

last impression 117
fine line 118
spy vs spy 119
starting over 120
don't for a minute 121
help from above 122
what now big guy 123
nation narcotic 124
weather report 125
is it over 126
the flight 127
too little too late 128
you got this 129
before it happens 130
mime 131
i have been away 132
the business of marriage 133
watch out 134
n word 135
makes no sense 136
50/50 love 137
adult toys 138
we remember don't you forget 139-140
in the cool of the day 141-143
adversity

the unexpected journey

opportunity

stewart sealy

the storm

your life is tossed
your hope lost at night
but your faith is not a shipwreck
all your emotions slip overboard
yet your life is spared
and a miracle pushes you ashore

time travel

with flowers in my hand from the future
i bend back time to see your face once more
i arrive
but you're not there

i must return before my memory of you is locked
away in the past

i sometimes hear your voice
but it seems so far away now
as though it travelled a long way
and faded before it could reach me across time

i still feel tempted to find you
but it costs to play with time

at the very least
i hope your travels are more successful than mine
but if for some strange reason you come looking
for me
you too must bend back time

nothing is what it seems

in lost there is found
in less there is more
in small there is great
in crisis there is opportunity
in blindness there is sight
in deafness there is sound
in noise there is silence
when alone there is presence

the struggle

zebras behind bars
of black and white

africa crying for life
half wasteland and modern cities
alike

the ancient sound of chains still in people's minds
children hiding
covered in dust

political cries that fall on deaf ears
money too good to resist

fathers hang on the past
mothers plant seeds
hoping that the children will see
a future that is beyond the trees

the struggle is still real
and the zebras are still not free

you be

starting small but thinking big
a great person in a small place
for the moment

a hero in a basket
a champion in the making
a king with no crown
a queen with no throne
wealthy without money
a gift with no wrapper

successful before seeing it
a good person with a broken heart
you've been given a lifetime to live in extraordinary
moments

addictions

if you are addicted to the opinions of others
you will overdose

if you are addicted to the approval of others
you will be co-dependent

if you are addicted to being controlled by others
you will become dysfunctional

addictions affect your destiny
they are all terminators sent from the future to kill
your identity
they never stop
not until your passion dies

the terminators want you terminated from living a
successful life
and it has crossed into your present
so that your future will never be
you must stop them now so that your dreams will
be a reality

seldom

we seldom know why
we seldom know how
we seldom know when
we seldom know where
we seldom know what
and we seldom know who

opportunity
the mystery at the door of expectation

the mystery

when that magic moment comes
and we no longer define ourselves by what we have
but more by the everlasting beings that we are
visible only in the nature of time
invisible to those that only look but do not see

when we lose something in our lives that only
connected us to a copy of something real
only then will we discover an eternal reality that
cannot be lost
and when we truly let go of something small
greatness can make its way into our lives

we shape our lives by the words that we speak now
the thoughts that we think today
and the actions that we dare to set in motion

imagine

imagine a world without you

a dance with no hand to hold
a smile with no face to see
a rose and no one to give it to
a flower cut in half
a moment of peace at last

the trick of the eye when i see you in the mirror
a painted picture in my mind
this is the only reflection i have of you now

the hot coffee clouds around the table
hiding our love at the evening café
the journey seems longer now without your aroma around

we enjoyed the magic of a life on the move
and the crazy times window shopping with plastic money
the secret looks peeping around the corner
and the body language that you don't learn in school

how do you replace a kiss with wine and tell stories with no audience

placing sticky notes on the wall to remember to forget you

it all seems so bizarre now
re-imagining a world without you
the mystery is that i have found a way to move on
this new journey is extraordinary

intelligent design

angels
if they are not real
man is a myth
and time created itself

humanity's next step is not an evolutionary one
but a resurrection to the original
not the copy

the choice of a new humanity
or by default
live with fallen angels adrift from divine reality

we
the copy of someone divine
the human struggle to define whether god or man
is blind
no big bang without an intelligent design
the telltale sign that a designer tailored this with his
mastermind

i saw the land called freedom
a paradise intelligently designed
it's humanity's final destiny
but will you see it in time

the crisis

dreams
just bits of thoughts framed in time
uttered words into history
stars buzzing by
drifting passions with no fixed future

hope given no purpose
like a bird with no tree to scan the landscape

my pen is empty of ink from writing someone else's story
the crisis of the times is in my decision to delay

the future

this magnetic pull on every born soul to be unique
as we journey out of time
the magic to make one's thoughts tangible
hand-held objects
our signature that we have been here
footsteps in the sand
lost in the wind
how i will be remembered in the future is up to me
but only if i make the decision to reconnect with
myself first

forward thinking

the thoughts that we think today will be the facts
that we live tomorrow
when you make today's thoughts about tomorrow's
dreams
it is easier to face tomorrow when you are living
your dreams today

when we don't value today
tomorrow will be of no value to us
and the future becomes nothing more than today's
thoughts of a better day

why you

it was not your smile
but your unseen tears
it was not your cold hands
but your warm heart
like flowers that needed water to come alive

your sophisticated steps reveal the rehearsals of
many nights dining out to dance
and long-forgotten moment of two people in love

the fragile relationships
like broken glass that can't be fixed
leftover memories of what was
like clowns smiling upside down

why you
i reasoned with time to turn back the clock
so that i could restart the past
put our love into an hourglass
and give it a second chance

i see the sparkle of your eyes
the windows to wishful thoughts
and words that will be remembered long after we
have danced our last dance

we spoke a language from a higher order that only
angels can understand

why you
because it was you
and only you

www

the tangible fibre-optics
the perfect spin for a spider looking for all of
humanity
this is the final frontier for an eight-legged predator
looking for lost souls

the footsteps
click-click like a tap dancer's secret code
revealing a brave new world
with creatures zipping by in cyberspace

passwords remembered forever in the cloud
we walk in the flesh
but we disappear in the net

the vibrations of travelling information is felt by
the spider's world-wide-web

now that you know you're never alone in the social
media
keep your identity to yourself
and your soul out of the world wide web
the spider is watching

baggage

i no longer need my past for mental or emotional
support
after all
who really cares

my shakespearean tragedy will not continue to be
acted out
unlike how the kings and queens in noble dresses
fall under the weight of inner stresses
there will not be a last scene of past baggage
following me

speak not of baggage to others in the flesh
the fickle mind judges in black and white
stand not in the courts of democratic minds that
cannot judge when your baggage is lost
never to be found

believe that the baggage of the past is out of sight
in the hustle and bustle of travel
resurrect now your new identity
and tell no tales of forgotten memories

red flower

the woman with the red flower has painted her face
for me
i have no secrets but just one
we are all aging

the bitter fruit was eaten
a long history we all must now face
sweet yes
but bitter to the taste

love can bypass the looking glass
to see the man with the red flower in his hand
and youth on his side

how i wish i had met her
not just behind the scene at a dress rehearsal
to tell her that i am real
how one word can change a destiny
this red flower
she shall never see
but she did paint her face for me

find the door

there is a door to somewhere better
it may be in the forest
and you may be standing at the crossroad
with an angel telling you not to fear

your only answer is not the pills to make sleep
forever
the betrayal is sharper than a knife
but so is the voice of forgiveness

some journeys seem long
but it's so that you can eventually find yourself

i found a pen
a key
and some memories
the second chance for true love
i imagine the words that i will write
and the key that will unlock what's right for me

find the door
behind it is another key to another door

free

if moments are free
i must not spend them on me

earth angels we must be
to help the blind see

i open doors with no key
if tomorrow is seen today
it's no longer a mystery

i have visions that have no limits placed on me
i create this moment that is free

can you see it

the world to come is far but its near
there the trees can hear
and the birds understand words
man and woman are back in the garden
the paradise lost is once again found
a thousand years like one day

all mysteries understood
like a body made of clay
the house for an earthly experience
by human spirits visiting a swiftly tilting planet

death
the invader to the everlasting
but out of a dying seed the secret of death's defeat

the world to come will turn the page
bent fingers will write straight
dim eyes will read the truth
as mankind awakens to the eternal news

this world slowly fading
the economics and resources running its course
the sun will shut itself down and end its shift
for another light will come into the world that is
brighter when you look in his face

the monster of fear

it lurks in the shadows
you can feel its presence on your skin
it whispers in your thoughts
and you'll never win

the enemy of positivity
the leader of hopelessness
the intruder that shuts doors to greatness

fear is the journey to the dark side
with well laid traps planted in the mind
the spooky moods of depression
and the pills for self-rejection
all done by a mere suggestion

it lives in the cities where pressure is high to leave a first impression
he knows you can't see him unless you look at your true reflection in the mirror
a little bat sitting on the left side
a visitor from the dark side
yet you can destroy fear with the echo location of self-identification

a hero

a hero stands on the street corner
in poverty
playing a violin
just like the great masters
he was once a dreamer of big things
but life happened to sink him like a defeated ship

we must not judge the music that sounds like a bad note
when life is off key
one day we will see servants riding horses
while princes are walking the streets

heroes are around us in strange clothing
they leave smiles behind for the brokenhearted
they put peace in confused minds
and they died with nails through their hands

heroes go unnoticed
every day
until you need a miracle to come your way

one day you will see heroes sitting on thrones
and princes standing on the corner
bewildered and in poverty
now playing a violin
and asking for spare change

the unexpected journey

in

ihumans

we have smart phones
drive smart cars
and live in smart homes
but read relationships for dummies

we can't hold hands because it feels funny
but we use plastic money
when did our online identity become more real
than our true humanity

we look for ihumans to replace machines that don't have to sleep
the new world order is ihumans that don't need to think

the ihumans will not arrive from women
but from automation

i am human

future minds

thoughts that travel no longer on paper or in books
but human stories from a glance or a look
x-ray eyes that read what's in the mind
ones resume from the shake of a hand
the new social crime is breaking past firewalls to get
to treasured thoughts

micro solar panels planted underneath the skin
access to renewable energy to stop aging
what are we walking around in
sticks for legs
levers to control
and pumps that we hope will not stop too early
before the bell tolls

we must move thoughts faster than the speed of
light
to keep our information from getting hacked
once dreams were reality
but reality is now a dream
when we replace this present mindset
will we be better off
or will we just hit delete

tea with a friend

we turn tables at our favorite cafe
flipping pages of thoughts like music ready to play
be it regrets lodged in the brain
broken relationships and of future love to find
the sleepover of memories that refuse to leave

the strange girl that enters the door that gets our attention
wondering what sort-of dragons we will have to fight as a noble knight
she hears the roar of a lamborghini and forgets our glances
we have a millionaire mind but no ideas or time
as she leaves with a coffee
we ponder how to buy her her dreams

the tea is a little cold now as we regather our thoughts
point our pens to notepads
and give it pressure to write about what didn't happen

the storm before the calm

you are never ready
but strange signs have been warning the
subconscious mind
the face you love blocks the calm before the storm

the low top
unbuttoned like a flash of revelation
but that's not for me
the unfamiliar perfume drifts in late at night
like a once familiar fog
now destroying lost ships

the ring that once sat as queen on that gentle hand
is now buried treasure for kings

hope now tossed on the sea of painful memories
not seeing the sun for a season
yet the promise of new love clears the fog on a
fresh page

if i had wealth

if i had wealth no one would be poor
i would heal the world
i would send world leaders to outer space and let
them drift
they talk like magic
but their pens gun down the poor and the middle
class left imprisoned
their economic policies can't even catch a wish

every year the same old paper hits the fan
and then taxes go up
and then jobs get cut

high school kids play a better game of chess than
the outer-space crew adrift
we now have eyes in the skies
funny space men watch for our crimes
like stealing bread to feed the birds before they are
dead
for they have dehumanized us with a pen
if i had wealth i would create the garden of eden
once again

drop the gun

drop the gun
don't take your life
love is knocking
at the door

yes
drugs pretended to be your friend
father left
and mom is working through the night

the love of your life
is in the club tonight
and you are not the guy on her mind

the street has no lights
drop the gun
don't take your life

wake up from this dream
she is knocking at the door
the one that understands your struggles

mom is working through the night
to give you a better life

year 3000

there is no more racism
the new humanity has all the spectrum of light in
the face of the true light

a new order of thinking
revelation that the history books left out
doctored by world oppressors

the ancient world gave the foundation of wisdom
that can't be stolen
for the universe has it written
guns
drugs
and slaves
some of the economics that made many rich is now
abolished

the government is no longer democratic
but a theocratic rule
taken from men and given to a new order of
humanity is now the truth
dusty men made of clay reshaped in a higher image

prayers won't get blocked by fallen angels
but will now clear the skies to heal the world
will we be here to see this new year

the fine line

i want to bend time to meet you once more
to square things up but it just doesn't bend
instead it leaves me with nightmares in the mirror
and on the mind
in the middle of fresh thoughts that have not found
their way into reality yet

i frame yesterday and hang it on the wall
and i let it tilt
not expecting perfection from an unsteady hand
we build with the substance of ideas
words and passions in action
the fragile relationships that remind us of glass

the long struggle to understand the aging of a rose
once picked
and the ending of a friendship while walking hand
in hand
i race home to look in the mirror
making sure that i am wearing a smile that doesn't
show my breaking heart

i try to remind myself to forget you
and i place sticky-notes to remember to

how one hidden letter found can act like a map
leading to the end of a long-shared journey
together

i take my last walk with eyes closed
hoping to run into you
but your perfumed presence is nowhere to be
found now
sometimes the message is not in a bottle that has
washed ashore
but in one's own heart
the first day of this unexpected journey

next time

the next time you see me
i will be the diamond that someone else has found
success won't be wishful thinking
or a collection of self-help quotes stuck on the
walls

my best revenge will be forgiveness and a wealthy
life
my body will be buffed
ya know
superman stuff
money won't sleep in my hands but will work the
midnight shift

a bullet can't stop an idea as hard as steel
king said i have a dream
this is not about black and white
it's about strong minds with a will to fight

next time you see me my empire will be built
it won't be something that you can see
positive thoughts will be surrounding me

i see relationships for what they are
broken people trying to heal
a day is not guaranteed
just the moment left that you have-to breathe

eternity makes no promises on earth

for even a flower must be plucked to give it away

if you find love don't clutter it with dark secrets
for evil hides when you let it

i once knew the joy of a life partner
but how quickly one can sink in sand
we all must let go of tangibles
be it people
places and things

left behind will be smiles
acts of kindness and miracles that others remember
you gave them as gifts
next time

keep life simple

life is simple until we complicate it
we clutter our minds with fear that moves like a fog
at night

we collect things as toys
and then cry when we lose them in the storms of
life

we sicken ourselves over what was not real in the
first place
i take not even my body of dust with me to the
grave
i put no clothes on lies to walk around like their
real

how a simple seed has the power to crack cement
so is the power that we possess to keep life simple
don't over complicate it

invisible

who told you that you are invisible

my body might not be here
powered by air
a network of intelligent design

moving subconsciously in a tangible shell
windows with lights to see

the legacy of books
songs and art
signs that i once was here
they tell no lies

forbidden fruit

we have already decided to take the fruit and share it
too smart for our own good
ended the future of freedom and manhood

now confused in space and time
searching for a peace of mind
she sees man as productivity and company
and he sees her as both a bitter fruit and a kiss of betrayal

the grass may be greener to closed eyes
and the hisses of snakes falls on deaf ears
a gold ring once dazzled her eyes
now a new man is her fantasy

i have met a new woman that speaks the truth and has a soul of virtue
even forbidden fruit must fall to the ground
with a bitter taste

a windy day

what does it mean to have a motivational mind
is it the choice to be positive in the face of
adversity
to stand firm
even with all the setbacks and unexpected journeys

it is clear to me that a motivational coach is not the
product of a classroom
but the baptism by fire weathered by storms
the true stories are found in the classroom of life
be the kind of coach that helps others outside the
room

ready

we are bigger than yesterday
for yesterday is gone

we are greater than today
for it shall pass

and we are larger than life
to face the future
for it will come

remember

age is not a factor for us
we transcend our bodies
we transcend wealth
and we transcend earth itself

the substance of dreams and visions have always
built great empires
and these great empires still speak to us from
beyond

why

the mind that is decided will cause the body to travel in the right direction
broken thoughts only add confusion to many avenues
once we find our why
the game changes
and winning is crossing the finish line first in our minds
and then we merely bring our bodies across

frog soup

do not
for a minute
wonder if you believe in yourself
in that moment
a seed of inferiority will take root
and you will have a tree of identity crisis giving you attitude
and frogs in your soup

wrong advice

limitation is the self-talk that we have anytime that we face an obstacle that informs us to heed the counsel of fear

electric blender

if you can't see beyond this moment
you will be blind to a lifetime of better ones

there is nothing permanent about the right-now
setbacks
few can gather positivity when negative emotions
are welcomed into the mix

alone

this feeling of being alone stops me from putting
on the lights at night
my room feels like a ten by ten cell
my phone is dead
and i can't call myself

i can hear the neighbor next door talking to himself
i am not the only one that is alone
i miss the shadow of the lady in my life

slowly i can eat again
and stop drinking my tears
where does loneliness come from anyway
and who would ever invent such a thing

i finally opened my door today
and this cell doesn't feel as much like a rabbit hole
i am not feeling so alone anymore

i never asked myself
why am i here
not until today
while watching some children play
i picked up my pen
a new-found friend
i started to write to myself as a pen-pal would
the way that children do
i won't be alone anymore

overtake

when we give our creative selves an assignment
ideas to do the impossible take over
and our subconscious that knows no limitations
causes the extraordinary to take place

once a thought loaded with positive energy emerges
empires from dream like blueprints
held in clay hands
shape the human experience

flowers on the bench

your eyes had no questions
and i had no answers
but i left flowers on the bench
roses just so you know

i hope that you sneak out at moonlight and wander
to the bench
stirred by long forgotten love that we once felt
before time said no

the beautiful red roses are my voice speaking to
your heart
i hope you seeing more than just stems and thorns
my hands are wondering where you are
and i hope these flowers will start a spark

if the flowers are still there in the morning
and the birds are not singing
then the letter that i sent you
to meet me
never reached its destination

just flowers on the bench

double meaning

you may feel alone in your adversity
but you are not forgotten
someone remembers you

you may be knocked down by the storms of life
but you are not destroyed
you may be feeling the pressure all around you
but you are not crushed

you may be disappointed
but it is only a set-up for a divine appointment

you may feel alone
but you are not abandoned

you may feel trapped
but really
you are only stepping into your freedom

paradox

we study
but are we smarter
we divide race
but are we not all human

we talk of freedom
but we still oppress each other
we have world wealth
but i still see the poor on every corner

we ask for truth
but our history books are distorted
we have lots of moments
but so little time
in the end
the shakers and the movers will be just dust along
with the street sweepers

different kind

i am empowered
invisible
and invincible

i have spiritual technology
i can stop bullets of lies
i can walk through walls
i can hear a feather in flight
and i can see stars fall

i am renewable energy
i am the new humanity of a higher order

indestructible
like the breeze

twenty-first century

the world is not about justice
it's not built on integrity
human beings will be the next commodity

are you marketable
profitable
can they make money
it's sad to say
but we live in a throw-away society

abortion is a scientific industry
cosmetic
human genetic
recycled personality
all pave the way to a dehumanizing economy

hey
safe sex is big business
repercussion played down by advertising clowns
just the other day i saw some kids out to play
they were reading girly books
so i looked the other way
with nothing to say
because they were the targeted market

when are we going to pick up the good-book and
take a look at ourselves
the reflection will be the truth in the face
jesus christ

died to save the human race

all we can think about is polluting space
automated office
software faces
plastic money
hey
the twenty-first century won't be very funny

your choice

whatever has been holding you back in life
is something you have accepted as a fact
masquerading
but no truth can be broken
and no lie can be binding

next level

strange thoughts

pigeons like the ground
and eagles like the sky

a small bad thought can poison a larger good one

a comfort zone has free parking
freedom is an investment
but slavery
the price of dignity
limitation is below infinity

price paid

you have a right to speak
you have paid for your story

the price was your pain
your struggles
and your identity

now
stand on the stage without a teleprompter
and let them read your life as they ponder

betrayal

betrayal has no face
it is not a person
it is a moving shadow that occupies space

it talks to those wanting forbidden fruit
sex
identity theft
and cyber-crimes

it sits beside beds like a black widow spider
watching the cheating soap opera
it is neither male nor female
but a living entity

drifting
looking for entertainment
it's only agenda
the shadow moves on to another victim with
forbidden fruit and a new mission

you got this

turn the clock back
give yourself time to imagine a new destiny

a body transformation
mental fitness
and a new set of positive emotions
understand your own creative self-help
and master your mind

okay the challenge

your greatness is untapped potential
undiscovered treasures
mysteries waiting to be revealed
undercover bosses
things yet to see
and things you have left to do

adventures still to take
other great people you must meet
and the wonders of your creative mind to release

permission to win

when you have-to start over
close chapters when they say the end
don't bring old characters to a new story

shut doors that have no exists
fear opening them again
and stop the insanity of the victim mentality

remember who you are
no one can give that to you

the stage

your presence in a room has a language of its own
less words are more

empower the space that you stand in
step into the opportunity
and slow time down

touch others in the room with positive energy
collect smiles
and put them in your memory

walk with command
but with a humble halo
and your presence will speak a language that others
will understand

all is not lost

a small idea is an empire that can be built

one dream starts a reality
when you hold a little key
it leads to a big door

an unexpected happening can turn into an epic discovery
the detour in the road connected you to finding new love

the misunderstood delay created the perfect timing
the impossible mission is now your assignment
the disappointment changed to an important appointment
a storm in your life pushed you ashore to a treasure island

upside down pages

we often look
but we rarely see

would you call that camouflage of you
or me

unexpected
a sudden happening that we were not prepared for
yet we know one thing is for sure
and that is change

redesigning your life
is coming to terms with what is no longer a reality
to allow for the extraordinary
a new awareness is upside down pages like these

when we find our why

when we find our why
we will stand on top of mountains

we will make paper planes fly
we will turn hate into love
cross the street to greet a black or white neighbor
we will take pictures with other cultures

when we find our why
we will take sand out of suffering oysters
and send gift cards instead of pearls

if we don't find our why
we will enslave for the sake of greed
we will make sure our money never sleeps
and pay four dollars a day to third world slaves

why did you read this today

know thy self

move in the direction that leads to your greatest success
even if it doesn't make sense to your mind
but it does to your heart

to get to the top of things
don't keep thinking of the bottom

too scared

a dance will sometimes be without the music
to hope you must take a chance
love is risky
but so is gambling

i want to see your eyes
but i have closed mine to hide the tears

i look to hold your hand once more
but i grab for a glass of wine
looking at life from a window
too scared to try to find the door

my pen is shaking
the words are not clear
let me spell it out
t-o-o-s-c-a-r-e-d-t-o-o-p-e-n-y-o-u-r-l-e-t-t-e-r

i already see the writing on the wall
and i am just too scared now
knowing that it's over

strange mystery

every person has been somewhere where they don't
belong
prophets in baskets
kings in caves
wise men in prisons
and god on the cross

the object of transportation
or the portal
is only the means to the end

prophets
the sender of words
kings with empires to build
wise men to lead the unlearned
and god to save the world

you have been given a unique journey
you have your own destiny unique to your
character
attitude
personality
and constitution

every time we move away from our purpose
we misplace our identity
if we define ourselves by society
then we create a tragedy

the unexpected journey

you have chapters assigned to you
a strange mystery
that's all i can say

secrets

truth
sunken treasures withheld
lies floating on top
tossed in the wind like confused thoughts

treasure maps to secrets
that i will never tell
going to the grave while she cast her spell

stolen kisses too late to forget
she has no regrets

lies too deep to find the truth
bits of yes and no mixed in the soul
overdose of confusion
there is no restitution

we should all be mutes
cause most people don't tell the truth
secrets

chips

don't chip your arm
the cameras will see
we can't buy or sell in this techno-political
economy

ultimate control of the soul is a slow train coming
smart houses and smarter cars
virtual vacations
corporations ruling the world
if we are chipped they will follow you
police your dreams
and reprogram your reality

this chip is not a trick
it's a tracking device in a cashless game of dice
access to our files with a voice
a new kind of slavery
like in the times of the pharaohs

now it won't be bricks and mortar we harvest
but the human soul
that is the real gold

they will put us on the assembly line
along with the robots
until we can't tell the time

drones follow us home
minds in the cloud picking us out in a crowd

this is not dr.seuss
it is revelations

agendas

redesigning your life is found in the understanding
that you have a say in what happens to you in the
chapters of your life
and how you control your response to the things
that you cannot control

we must not believe that we are victims of
circumstances
in fact
circumstances are not intelligent happenings on
their own
they are designed by thinking agents
wanting to enforce their agendas over your own

pieces of yesterday

my thoughts will become my words
my words will become my thoughts
speeding pieces of energy
waves leaving my being
finding a place in this world

something must be said about our human worth

my thoughts are thinking
and my words are asking questions

the world is like a sandbox
build your castles
i am in my own prison
and the keys are in my pocket
the past is nothing more than a place you have
been

parallel

i wake to a parallel universe
there is another me
my best version of myself
imposter
i yell

impossible
i contemplate

i face me in the parallel universe
but i can't find where i am hiding that other part of myself

only to discover that both universes are within me
my best version is two in one
not half looking for someone else

brown sugar

born in paradise
belize
brown sugar islands floating on the blueberry
coloured caribbean sea

mayan history for a backyard
a jungle playground
slow moving turtles
water taxis for curious birds
the breeze is lazy on the beach
mango skins smelling so sweet
girls bobbing in the sea to reggae caribbean beats
born in paradise

belize

all
_____

frozen

can't move
time is stuck

i want to let you go
but i am frozen

around the corners i catch glimpses of you
or is it just my holographic thoughts racing ahead
hoping

i want to let you go
but i am frozen
i am stuck
in time

a strange day

felt like it was the end of the world
the perfect storm of life with no exit door
pulled my mood out of a hat
tricked myself into being happy
what a day

the paper hit the fan
the wine stopped me from drinking when the
bottle went missing
i pick up the bible
and found moses drifting on the sea
a little one sleeping in a manger
a strange day
not only for me

who can tell

i dance in the face of fear
i lift my faith in a heavy moment
knowing a path will appear

in the wilderness
i pick up a walking stick
a companion that knows hardship

the chapters of my life are just beginning
eternity is near

the stars that abraham counted
a sign that nations would appear
sadness that turns to joy
save your life and lose it
lose your life and gain it
who can tell

you don't understand

i am okay
i know that math won't figure this out

i must choose to live my passion
or the box will imprison me
even the prophets didn't understand their own destinies

i don't need a pen to spell it out
i have been to the mountain top
and i have walked in the wilderness
i have seen angels and god sitting

but who am i
but a prophet seeing

the last day

celebrate
have no regrets
the problem of pain
hung on the cross
speak with your eyes
dance with joy inside
all is not lost
love is the final language that we all will understand

framed

i am on the wall
cornered and hanging
i have been framed

i see your every move
and it's off the wall

you left me hanging
once admired
once desired
and now you leave me tilted and abandoned

i feel the years now
your shadow blocks my escape
and i am still here on the wall
cornered and hanging

i have been framed

secrets again

what we don't say is what hurts
the things that we do say come far too late
even a spider knows not to get caught in its own
web

we hold onto our own secrets
but in the end
all of our secrets become dirty laundry

she had a secret to tell her lover
but she found a desperate power in keeping it
until the fruit turned rotten to the sound

the truth fell from the tree
in this game that we play that nobody can ever win
the yes that means no
and the no that means yes
is this a relationship

our love is spelled out on the chessboard
checkmate
or is this our fate

confusing secrets
this maze that i walk through
just to get to you

bleeding doves

no one sees when doves cry
a broken heart speaking in their eyes

when doves fly
it's no question why
moving on is just a matter of choice

only another bleeding dove can hear that cry
broken wing
or broken heart
pick up this bleeding dove

talking drums

we played drums in our chains
we
the slaves
tap danced as a way to speak to one another
the only voice that we heard

we worked hard to master the trade
cause one day we're gonna to be free

stealing with our eyes
we sent morse code messages with winks
we got charged for crimes in the blink of an eye
a small price to pay for the next generation to be
free

ghetto

the state of this environment leaves an imprisoned
psyche
a reflection of what i see inside
make-believe comes true
if the ghetto is your graffiti school
skip class to run street business
its all about who rules

sure
i would love to wear a business suit like mr.clean
but out here guns settle the score
we all want out of the ghetto
but who is going to make it policy

stop fooling yourself
the ghetto makes the economy flow
it's all on paper
the budget is fixed
and that's how government business goes

puppets

they said no strings attached
but here i am now
still boxed in with the same old tax
everyone knows that we are all called jack-in-the-
box

dust yourself off

looking buff
eating well again
i am not throwing packages of chicken breasts
away because it went bad anymore
no more wasting good money
but i just didn't feel liking cooking for only myself
i was so used to cooking for the family
and that was so cool
i guess i went into shock when i found myself
alone

some battles are over-eating
and others are hardly eating at all
both are a losing war

well
people do us favours when they exit our lives
when smiles go bad
hearts now cold
and the magic has gone south

you do the math and divide what's yours
once the shock wears off a year later
you weigh your options
you pull out your survival list
and you dust yourself off

is this for real

the journey goes far deeper that you can imagine
it's spiritual
economical
visible and the unseen

the good well meaning
the bad intentional
and the ugly that's forceful

the journey is demanding
and taxing
and dropping the ball in relationships

taking masks off
the revealing

rings will lose their meaning
words will splash back in your face
misunderstandings will be settled in courts
friends will part
and enemies will gather
at the worst times you will have to stand alone
we step on snakes of fear

finding strength when you are out of breath
running from oneself
taking back your dignity
believing you are up when you are down
trust you have found your way when seeing the

fork on the road

defend yourself from mental voices of doubt
make your bed in your car
and staying awake fighting invisible monster to your
success

escape from your middle earth
resist temptations to settle for the good
and wait for the best

black privilege

ageless
and you can't tell
inventors of great civilizations
masters of philosophy and poetry
wise men from the east
noble kings and queens
the last shall be first once again
overcoming evil with good
a war of words
you just got served

mistake

don't mistake kindness as weakness
and don't mistake power as greatness
kindness is power over weakness
and greatness is kindness in weakness

executive decision

i live repercussions
so
this an executive decision
i am not interested in negative opinions

this is not a democratic decision
i am moving in a new direction
and this will be a successful resurrection

got a new attitude on
dressed in gratitude
and the ceo of my soul

i am in business for success
left the past behind
and dropped the glass of wine
and it is now about a healthy mind

glad you stepped out of my life
happy that it now feels right
bodybuilding my own body
man
i am looking jacked

i thought that i couldn't do it without you
but surprise
it's not true

i speak motivation to my crew

the unexpected journey

aboard the executive jet that has my name
the power of how i now think has my book in ink
how did all this happen so fast
it was an executive decision
first class

the last day of my past

well
i just got evicted from my past

i have one day to pack my mental stuff
and dump my baggage

i am moving out from this neighbourhood of
doom and gloom

this is the last day of my past
and i am returning the keys back to the dark side

i was living next to some scary characters
like one named *trapped*
and another that goes by the name *depression*

a higher power evicted me out of love
i am now moving to a new neighbourhood
so excited about who i am
what i am doing
and where i am going

you too should move if you are living in a bad
neighbourhood
and then make it the last day of your past

relationship

two souls that left eternity that never met
to have an earthy experience

time said okay the stage is set
the circumstances are now in place
time to start a new story
let us begin with a spark
new chemistry
and then we move to compatibility

they will spend earthly time together
helping each other to reach their full potential
we will give them rings to remind them that they
are committed to one another
when they forget
they will have their vows
as they grow old
and the number of days in the book ends

they will have created lots of memories
and they will both look back on their full potential

four years later

i wish you well
no ulterior motives or ill meant
life is too short
and i am doing great
our kids are men now
and living their dreams that we both helped to
create

we should be proud of how their lives turned out
yes
the mirror broke
and the reflection of love distorted
but that was not what they should see
forgive and forget i think go together
if i remember the lessons found in sunday school

regrets
we all shall have some
yet its four years later now
and i choose to be happy

persuasion

just when you're about to have a breakthrough
an obstacle comes to block you
distractions often happen in threes

this is where positive mental power comes into
being

many are conditioned to back down
easy to follow the crowd
if this set of adversity disturbs you
how will you get to the next level
the test is to see if you really want uncommon
dreams
or an average reality

today
if you want to be elite
the risk must be without reservation

there can be no refinement
unless there is self-persuasion
the conclusion is
there is no illusion
if you want to win

divine balance

one will arrive by birth
and journey out of time

one will plant something
and others will sit under the shade of it

a dream will die for a season
yet healing will come from it

there is a time to break down walls that divide
and to build new relationships

even a face must weep
and a face must laugh
grieving will come
and so will dancing for joy

you will throw stones away
and you will pick them up again when you must
there is a moment of warm embrace
and knowing the time not to embrace

there will be times of gain
and other times there will be loss
wisdom will tell you to keep
and wisdom will tell you to let go

things need to tear
and things will need to be sewn

someone must stand up and speak out
and someone needs to embrace silence

the moment for love will present itself
and the moment to hate will be clear
war will become necessary
and peace will have its opportunity

lion in the street

the city talks at night
stories on every corner
dancing shoes tapping
music jamming
lights are blinding
as the lion is hiding
beggars are carving and pan handling
the city is alive
not many dreams changing lives
money can't sleep because of the noise
as the lion is hiding
the night is young
but the city is old
as the lion is hiding
it is the weekend
the craziness begins
people are forgetting the business of thinking
as the lion is hiding

no rush

take your time
but hurry up
i have my feelings on the clock

are we doing friendship
or romance
no rush

i have escaped reality
i have been lost in the forest and i can't see the
trees
darkness like a witch is haunting me
no rush
reaching for your hand
hope it's the real deal

take your time
but hurry up

game of hearts

who will sit on the throne of you heart
is it me
or him

you hold the cards

i seek a dragon to slay to impress you
but he found the keys to your heart
and you hold the cards

i gave you the head of the dragon
but he stole a ring
and brought flowers that cost him nothing
but you hold the cards

final love

i fear that time has aged my hope
the age-a-phobia graffiti is now a mentality

society doesn't like old age
we mock the aging process
and we find old homes to send them to
strangers don't feed them well
and they pretend they have friends

these are real people that still pay old taxes
serving the system as good employees
now that they are unproductive
and taking up space
we now send them to waste in a unhappy place
called old age

i look for final love
and i pick a number out of hat

it seems too late
so many are set in their ways
when i am young again
i will find my final love

she

she walked into the room
heads turned
sparks flew
she took our breath away
and we couldn't breath
that girl was dangerous

we all fell to our knees
but she looked at me
i knew that i had to leave
the danger was too real

she caused the lights to dim with one move
that night i could not sleep
trying to break the spell
she was that dangerous
what the hell

in the hood

brooklyn new york
guns are heavy
kids running
and bullets fly with no wings

nameless faces
this is the hood
gangs with turf
tattoo body language
streets all red
and kids are lying dead

life in the hood
this is no red-riding hood
school bell rings
and the turf wars begins

crews all trying to be slick
ai smarter than these kids
everyone locks their doors
this is the hood

we bring soldiers home
no more kids left behind in the hood

glitter but is it gold

that guy has money
but do you only want to be his honey
without no ring
you are just a playboy bunny

he has all the bells and the whistles
but in a character deficit

you can't just wing it
love should be for life

the lambo is breathtaking
i get it
he is just playing
find someone that is true
and god will bless you

reach

every day should be another exciting day
we get to think bigger thoughts
we get to reach a little higher than yesterday
we get to drop more limitations
and we get to see beyond this moment

dreams look a lot more real
impossible
sounds like possible
and the storms seem to make us stronger

we rise with a cutting-edge mentality
breaking through negativity

excited about where we are heading
it's all about prosperity

flipside

when you have power
you need purpose
and when you have purpose
you will need power

missing in action

the box looked so cold
i knew you were in there
but soon to be dust

you had courage under fire
as a soldier must
while battling cancer

shots fired
hope hit the giant
as he went down in remission
homie
i know you're doing the night shift in a better place

you are missing in action
but we will remember your name

earth angel

blue ocean eyes
black hair riding the wind in a storm
everyone standing outside on the street corner
waiting to cross

an earth angel in my midst
saved me from a near miss
you left so fast
that all i remember is your blue ocean eyes
and my silent thank you
echoing in the wind

inner world

we often fear our thoughts
we don't always know what to do with them
they seem to wander
aimless like a ship without a sail
we are afraid of dark thoughts
thinking they are invaders from a past life

we hope they will leave
like a stranger knocking at a door needing help
they seem to suddenly flood our lives without any
warning

at times
we answer them
as if talking to a friend
i know that some thoughts can push us to the end

words unspoken
take up space
and must be released
or they can have internal repercussions
and only a pen can capture the thoughts
that a broken heart cannot

no one left

the trees listen
what have they heard

stories hidden
treaties broken
many hid behind them from slave traders
they have seen men come and go
for thousands of years

living longer than all of mankind put together
we cut down trees
we will never see again
no shade for the next generation

last impression

i saw the lion with gentle eyes
the smell of lavender moved in with a breeze
the sick
the blind
and the crippled
were healed by his shadow

in a simple way
all i saw was his reflection
and it was my last impression

fine line

balance of now
and eternity
what will we do with destiny

animated in the now
yet to dust we must bow

the mirror is getting brighter
but we are fading
ancient knowledge to grab
but no time for contemplation

the line is fine
but one day
there will be a better you and i

spy vs spy

i chased you
and you chased me
in virtual reality

you kept disappearing to another galaxy
looking for love
is this your idea of a spy game
are you real
or just a fake personality
trick or treat
i thought you were into me

i tried to delete this game
but now it feels all too real now
i saw you running through the crowd

why are we spying on each other
when we are both looking for true love
let us meet outside this game
and rekindle this flickering flame

starting over

the puzzle hit the floor
a thousand pieces of my heart
some land under that bed where we once said i love you
others end up in dark places
others
i fear
i will never find

i want them back all in one box

don't for a minute

don't for a minute think this is over
i still have to bottle my tears
i have to gather my thoughts and emotions
and repackage them again
i still have to buy a new heart
for a second chance at finding love
so
this is far from being over

help from above

i am happier now
i don't know how i managed that

it was so hard organizing my emotions
and filing my thoughts into a positive collection
i wondered if aging would scare new love away
many forgotten faces once beauty fades
what a superficial world around us
i pull out my dumbbells and make my body young again
everyone wants to know how old everyone is
but few want to know have you truly lived

i don't care too much now about impressing others
for after all this
i must impress myself first
i wanted to ask myself what happened
how did i get out of that dark place
it really was very dark
sadness is not for champions
and the truth is
i had help from above

what now big guy

the broken bottle
the wet letter
my cut figure
blood on the sand

this spot we often came to
to watch the waves come in

wish i was alone
but i can't make the stars disappear
too much light to read by

what's the deal with poetry
just say it
it doesn't have to rhyme
it simply says you've moved on

nation narcotic

smoke the kids away
let us all pretend this is a video game
bullets don't have no names
the crossfire ends teenage scholarships

we at nine to five
glass houses with empty rooms
but the grass looks fine
doesn't matter if this stuff won't last

terrible thing to lose a mind
lots of studying
and now we have smart cars

characters behind bars for small dimes
but the leaf is legalized
we have it all wrong
this thing we call relationship
one text and it's ended

which man is in the mirror now
and which women is cinderella
and who has her glass slipper
let us get our kids back on track
let us put meaning back in our relationships
and stop the narcotics

weather report

the fog is clearing up in my mind
no pills taken
or strong drink

sun is back shining in my heart
blue skies painting a smile
a warm breeze of hope has me believing in love
again
no more turbulence ahead
if i fly tonight toward a brighter day
i will arrive with peace
for i know
i have the weather report

is it over

i have the memory still
but without the pain

the flight

two birds were flying at forty thousand feet
suddenly
one bird had to make a crash landing
and the other just kept flying south

too little too late

a little drama
a little wine
and just too much time to think

you got this

detection
apprehension
frustration
depression
and investigation

put down the glass of wine
forgiveness
be divine

reflection
self-help identification
start new
this is for you

before it happens

i see things happen before they do
i have a short window into time
pieces moved on the chessboard
i see where this is going
no checkmate in this game

this is not the science of movement
or divinci-code
this is just your way of playing the game

mime

We have said so many things to each other without
words
let us stop guessing
hoping the message is clear

i still don't understand
even when we held hands

the street clowns watch us
as we walk by wondering
if what we are doing is mime

the beautiful thing about you
is that your eyes
they tell the truth

i have been away

i understand the rusty nails in your hands now
love will make us do what most just like reading about
one that takes a bullet for a friend

fighting a dragon to reach her
the long travel to find that pot of gold
showing up nine to five until one grows old
bottling that letter
and sending it to sea
sos

my face finally has a smile
my hands are finally warm from holding yours
the bullet is out
the dragon is dead
and i have a pot of gold
and the letter has been read
i am finally with the one that i truly love

the business of marriage

the kiss feels purchased
did i get my moneys worth

i signed all the paperwork
how can you leave

i cut the grass
yet you looked in another yard

i put my money in the pot
and you had make-up
dresses
and a car

we went for country walks
but your mind was so far away

what's love got to do with it was playing in your car
then i realized that you are a business-women
and you terminated the contract in your heart
and then you hit send

watch out

they fell from a higher order of life
landed on earth
wings burnt on the way down
they live invisible to the sight
they collect souls
not committed to christ
this is not philosophy
it is spiritual reality
end of day
we all have a choice
light or dark
watch out

n word

children rush to play
multicultural games
colorblind to lies
they all know we are all the same
they use the word neighbours
and aren't we our brothers keeper

we learn life lessons with fun and games
teaching adults to play multicultural neighbours
so the n word
is neighbours
i hear the children
say

makes no sense

i ponder human fascination with material things as
a status
the birds are royally dressed and penniless
the flowers all have make-up and a great attitude
even when we pull them from their home

bees work hard to share their honey
and we are busy
trying to be better than another man
the stars have never been to school
yet
they teach knowledge without any rules
we love
the symbols more than the person
watch as they start aging
we forget the beauty inside
and we
start trading

her body is soft for now
but
shortly the mirror will tell the truth
and will whisper
she is wrinkling
a crazy thought drifts in
saying
define yourself by material things

50/50 love

two sides to a coin
yours and mine
yet one
to spend it together
sorry
for not seeing your tears
when the lights were off
i should have sat up that night
and shared our fears
i wanted to help you forget the past
it was so deep
so i put it off
sorry for dropping the ball
when you needed me at
that sensitive time

i wrote you a letter
i almost sent it
instead i hit delete
i had my own internal battles

i wanted to say i really love you
sorry
is it too late

adult toys

we entertain pride and prejudice
we celebrate being set in our ways
yet we tell children to grow up
and stop playing games

we say sticks and stones
but we know calling names will hurt another
we still watch soap operas
and betray each other

we click goodbye in seconds
on online dating
with no clue about someone else's story

your christmas tree may be empty
in the morning
we are not speaking about sex toys
we are talking about receiving
the gift of honouring
compassion and blessings
for these are the true rewards

the unexpected journey

we remember don't you forget

i begged silently in prayer for one more second of
another intelligent conversation with our mother
i listen to her struggle to balance the two persons
within her

the evening has set in and she is half home
my name flickers between son and my given name

a traffic of workers pass by her in the nursing
home
each a blur to memory cells shutting down for the
night
her voice is both mother and patient saying
help me
this is not right

i try to rush the call for the pain has stained me
a helpless son so far away hurts me

i look upwards in my room and wonder where have
all the miracles gone
i see the shadow alzheimer claim another

i think of ships lost at sea and how lighthouses on
the shore guide them home
when all hope seems lost
her faith is her lighthouse that will
one day
guide her home from the shadow while she is half

home
on the sea

you never gave your kids away struggling as a single
mother
i sold bottles to buy milk and bread while you
worked three jobs to get ahead
was no fun being black and unwed in those days
and we saw your tears trying to be both mother and
father
we thank you
you never failed

we know the time will come when you are no
longer on the phone
we then will know that you are finally home

(dedicated to our mother merlene)

in the cool of the day

in the cool of the day i communed with a prophet
and his words were like electric currents that
resuscitated my soul

he told me
son come sit on the edge of tomorrow and listen to
what i have to say
long ago i tried in vain to convince my shadow to
go out in front of me
from fear of having to choose at the crossroads
between the broad and narrow
but i let pharaoh go in the end
cause the first will be last and the second
i accepted that
i found myself on the unbeaten path

knee deep in a sinkhole of self-doubt
questioning if this was even the right route
what with a world that doesn't want to walk this
way
they rather add stains than abstain
throw all the paint on the wall
and say you don't have to subtract when it's
abstract
but truly i tell you
if the grey really matters
then you'll see it's black and white

now imagine one night

your mural masterpiece is defaced
and however hard you try to peel off the paint
you realize at some point it has to be replaced
so
after an epic chase in which you track down the vandal and handle him
you begin anew on a blank canvas
and if i'm candid
every predicament
past and future-present stems from this very moment

now my motive in telling you this is 'cause we're paintbrushes
but as long as there's a thorn in your soul
even in the hands of the most masterful
you'll be difficult to hold
so much so few eyes will see and ears will hear that these living words you speak are actually a mirror

but remember just as you once ran from your real reflection
so too will others flee when they see themselves so clearly
cause at first stare the spots wrinkles and blemishes are there
but the longer you look the truest you begins to appear

a person of purpose divinely designed
sent from the sky
the spoken word of the most high

zie
you're here to remind others why they're alive
and that is your deadline

(to my dad from zaire)

stewart sealy

adversity

Manufactured by Amazon.ca
Bolton, ON